Where Animals Live

Animals in the Arctic

By John Wood

KidHaven PUBLISHING

Published in 2018 by
KidHaven Publishing, an Imprint of Greenhaven Publishing, LLC
353 3rd Avenue
Suite 255
New York, NY 10010

© 2018 Booklife Publishing
This edition is published by arrangement with Booklife Publishing.

All rights reserved. No part of this book may be reproduced in any form without permission in writing from the publisher, except by a reviewer.

Designer: Matt Rumbelow
Editor: Holly Duhig

Photo credits: Abbreviations: l-left, r-right, b-bottom, t-top, c-center, m-middle. Images are courtesy of Shutterstock.com, with thanks to Getty Images, Thinkstock Photo, and iStockphoto. 2 - Denis Burdin, 3 - Denis Burdin, 4 - Ritesh Chandhary, 5tl - sirtravelalot, 5m - Lenar Musin, 5mr - Longjourneys, 5bl - Scott E Read, 5br - Fish Ho Hong Yun, 6 - ginger polina bublik, 7- Jamen Percy, 8 - DonLand, 9 - Galyna Andrushko, 10 - outdoorsman, 11 - Amelie Koch, 12 - Incredible Arctic, 13 - Paul Reeves Photography, 14 - Karelian, 15 - Martin Hejzlar, 16 - CampCrazy Photography, 17 - Miles Away Photography, 18 - Sergey Uryadnikov, 19 - Helen Birkin, 20 - Yulia YasPe, 21 - Jan Martin Will, 22 - Jo Crebbin, 23 - Vladimir Wrangel

Cataloging-in-Publication Data

Names: Wood, John.
Title: Animals in the arctic / John Wood.
Description: New York : KidHaven Publishing, 2018. | Series: Where animals live | Includes index.
Identifiers: ISBN 9781534523838 (pbk.) | 9781534523807 (library bound) | ISBN 9781534525160 (6 pack) | ISBN 9781534523821 (ebook)
Subjects: LCSH: Animals–Antarctica–Juvenile literature.
Classification: LCC QL106.W66 2018 | DDC 591.9989–dc23

Printed in the United States of America

CPSIA compliance information: Batch #CW18KL: For further information contact Greenhaven Publishing LLC, New York, New York at 1-844-317-7404.

Please visit our website, www.greenhavenpublishing.com. For a free color catalog of all our high-quality books, call toll free 1-844-317-7404 or fax 1-844-317-7405.

CONTENTS

Page 4 — What Is a Habitat?
Page 6 — What Is the Arctic?
Page 8 — Types of Arctic Habitat
Page 10 — Walruses
Page 12 — Arctic Terns
Page 14 — Lemmings
Page 16 — Beluga Whales
Page 18 — Polar Bears
Page 20 — The Arctic in Danger
Page 22 — Endangered Animals
Page 24 — Glossary and Index

Words that look like *this* can be found in the glossary on page 24.

WHAT IS A HABITAT?

A habitat is a place where an animal lives. It provides the animal with food, shelter, and everything else it needs to survive.

a polar bear on the Arctic ice

There are many different habitats in the world. Each one is home to several different animals.

forests

deserts

oceans

mountains

rain forests

WHAT IS THE ARCTIC?

The Arctic is an area around the North Pole which is very cold. It is made up of the Arctic Ocean and all the land around it.

The North Pole

The Arctic is home to many animals. In the winter, it can become too cold for some animals so they move south. This is called migration.

These are the northern lights, which sometimes appear in the Arctic sky.

TYPES OF ARCTIC HABITAT

Many Arctic animals live on sea ice. In the cold winter, there is more sea ice. In the warm summer, some of this ice melts or breaks away.

sea ice

Some animals live on land, in the Arctic tundra. There are no trees in the tundra because the ground is too cold. Only small shrubs and plants can grow.

tundra

WALRUSES

Walruses are often found lying on the edge of sea ice, or swimming in the Arctic Ocean. They live in big groups with hundreds of other walruses.

a group of walruses

Walruses are able to stay warm because of the blubber in their bodies. They need this blubber to stay warm in the cold waters.

ARCTIC TERNS

Arctic terns make their homes in the tundra. They dig nests on the ground called scrapes. This is where they look after their *young*.

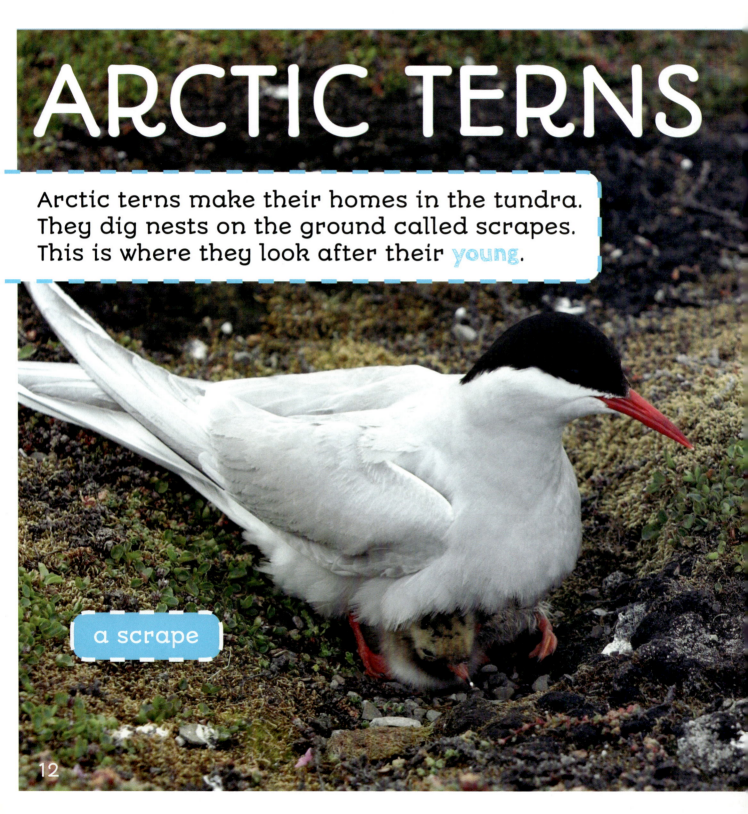

a scrape

Arctic terns don't live in the Arctic all year. In the winter, they migrate to Antarctica.

Arctic terns migrate farther than any other animal.

LEMMINGS

Lemmings make their homes in underground burrows in the tundra. Their burrows are made up of many different tunnels all joined together.

A lemming peeks out of its hiding place.

Sometimes too many lemmings are born at the same time. When this happens, large groups of lemmings will migrate to find a new home with more food.

BELUGA WHALES

Beluga whales live in the Arctic Ocean, near the coast. They migrate south when the Arctic Ocean becomes too icy in the winter.

beluga whale

A group of beluga whales is called a pod. There are often around 10 whales in a pod. They talk to each other by chirping, clicking, and whistling.

pod of beluga whales

POLAR BEARS

Polar bears live on the Arctic ice. Their white fur makes them harder to see against the ice. This helps them sneak up on their prey.

Female polar bears make dens in the snow. This is where they raise their cubs. Polar bears usually have two cubs.

a polar bear cub in its den

THE ARCTIC IN DANGER

When harmful gases from cars, airplanes, and factories go into the air, they trap heat on Earth and cause the planet to warm up. This is called global warming, and it is putting Arctic animals in danger.

Global warming melts sea ice in the Arctic. This makes it harder for some animals to survive. When an animal is finding it hard to survive, it is said to be endangered.

ENDANGERED ANIMALS

RINGED SEALS

Some types of ringed seals are endangered. Because global warming is melting the sea ice, many seals have nowhere to live and raise their young.

SIBERIAN CRANES

During the Arctic summer, Siberian cranes live in the tundra. But as the world gets warmer, the cold tundra is disappearing. This means Siberian cranes have less space to look for food.

GLOSSARY

blubber — a thick layer of fat under the skin of sea mammals, such as whales and seals

burrow — a hole or tunnel dug by an animal

coast — the area where the land meets the sea

den — an animal's home, dug in earth or snow

endangered — when a species of animal is in danger of going extinct

gas — an air-like substance that expands freely to fill any space available

prey — animals that are hunted by other animals for food

sea ice — seawater that freezes into ice, which is often slightly salty

shelter — protection from danger and harsh weather

tundra — a cold area where trees do not grow

young — an animal's offspring

Index

cold 6–9, 11, 23
endangered 21–22
food 4, 15, 23
global warming 20–22
ice 4, 8, 10, 18, 21–22
melt 8, 21–22
migrate 7, 13, 15–16
summer 8, 23
tundra 9, 12, 14, 23
water 11
winter 7–8, 13, 16
young 12, 22